SELF LOVE
JOURNAL
Book Club

THIS JOURNAL BELONGS TO:

DAILY SELF LOVE JOURNAL

Mood: 😞 😟 😐 🙂 😃　　　Date:

Empowering affirmation

I feel good about myself because...

Today, I forgive myself for...

Reflection

Reminder

WEEKLY SELF LOVE JOURNAL

Mood: 🙁 😞 😐 🙂 😀　　　Date:

Monday

Three positive things about me...

Tuesday

I feel good about myself when...

Wednesday

Things I should do when I'm sad...

Thursday

Things I should do when I'm Bored...

WEEKLY SELF LOVE JOURNAL

Mood: ☹ ☹ 😐 ☺ 😃   Date:

Friday

Things I should do when I feel tired...

Saturday

Things that made me happy today...

Sunday

I will challenge myself to...

Notes:

DAILY SELF LOVE JOURNAL

Mood: 😣 😦 😐 🙂 😄   Date:

Empowering affirmation

I feel good about myself because...

Today, I forgive myself for...

Reflection

Reminder

WEEKLY SELF LOVE JOURNAL

Mood: ☹ ☹ ☺ ☺ ☺   Date:

Monday

Three positive things about me...

Tuesday

I feel good about myself when...

Wednesday

Things I should do when I'm sad...

Thursday

Things I should do when I'm Bored...

WEEKLY SELF LOVE JOURNAL

Mood: ☹ ☹ 😐 ☺ 😄   Date:

Friday

Things I should do when I feel tired...

Saturday

Things that made me happy today...

Sunday

I will challenge myself to...

Notes:

DAILY SELF LOVE JOURNAL

Mood: ☹ ☹ 😐 ☺ 😀   Date:

Empowering
affirmation

I feel good about
myself because...

Today, I forgive
myself for...

Reflection

Reminder

____

____

____

____

____

____

____

____

WEEKLY SELF LOVE JOURNAL

Mood: ☹ ☹ 😐 ☺ 😄   Date:

Monday

Three positive things about me...

Tuesday

I feel good about myself when...

Wednesday

Things I should do when I'm sad...

Thursday

Things I should do when I'm Bored...

WEEKLY SELF LOVE JOURNAL

Mood: ☹ ☹ 😐 🙂 😃   Date:

Friday

Things I should do when I feel tired...

Saturday

Things that made me happy today...

Sunday

I will challenge myself to...

Notes:

DAILY SELF LOVE JOURNAL

Mood: ☹ ☹ 😐 🙂 😄   Date:

Empowering affirmation

I feel good about myself because...

Today, I forgive myself for...

Reflection

Reminder

WEEKLY SELF LOVE JOURNAL

Mood: 🙁 🙁 😐 🙂 😃   Date:

Monday

Three positive things about me...

Tuesday

I feel good about myself when...

Wednesday

Things I should do when I'm sad...

Thursday

Things I should do when I'm Bored...

WEEKLY SELF LOVE JOURNAL

Mood: ☹ ☹ 😐 ☺ 😄   Date:

Friday

Things I should do when I feel tired...

Saturday

Things that made me happy today...

Sunday

I will challenge myself to...

Notes:

DAILY SELF LOVE JOURNAL

Mood: ☹ ☹ 😐 🙂 😃   Date:

Empowering affirmation

I feel good about myself because...

Today, I forgive myself for...

Reflection

____

____

____

____

Reminder

____

____

____

____

WEEKLY SELF LOVE JOURNAL

Mood: 😟 😦 😐 🙂 😃   Date:

Monday

Three positive things about me...

Tuesday

I feel good about myself when...

Wednesday

Things I should do when I'm sad...

Thursday

Things I should do when I'm Bored...

WEEKLY SELF LOVE JOURNAL

Mood: ☹ ☹ ☺ ☺ ☺   Date:

Friday

Things I should do when I feel tired...

Saturday

Things that made me happy today...

Sunday

I will challenge myself to...

Notes:

DAILY SELF LOVE JOURNAL

Mood: 😟 😦 😐 😊 😄   Date:

Empowering affirmation

I feel good about myself because...

Today, I forgive myself for...

Reflection

Reminder

WEEKLY SELF LOVE JOURNAL

Mood: 🙁 ☹️ 😐 🙂 😃   Date:

Monday

Three positive things about me...

Tuesday

I feel good about myself when...

Wednesday

Things I should do when I'm sad...

Thursday

Things I should do when I'm Bored...

WEEKLY SELF LOVE JOURNAL

Mood: ☹ ☹ ☺ ☺ ☺   Date:

Friday

Things I should do when I feel tired...

Saturday

Things that made me happy today...

Sunday

I will challenge myself to...

Notes:

DAILY SELF LOVE JOURNAL

Mood: ☹ ☹ 😐 ☺ 😃   Date:

Empowering affirmation

I feel good about myself because...

Today, I forgive myself for...

Reflection

Reminder

___________________   ___________________

___________________   ___________________

___________________   ___________________

___________________   ___________________

WEEKLY SELF LOVE JOURNAL

Mood: ☹ ☹ 😐 ☺ 😃   Date:

Monday

Three positive things about me...

Tuesday

I feel good about myself when...

Wednesday

Things I should do when I'm sad...

Thursday

Things I should do when I'm Bored...

WEEKLY SELF LOVE JOURNAL

Mood: 😞 😦 😐 🙂 😄   Date:

Friday

Things I should do when I feel tired...

Saturday

Things that made me happy today...

Sunday

I will challenge myself to...

Notes:

DAILY SELF LOVE JOURNAL

Mood: 😟 😦 😐 🙂 😃   Date:

Empowering affirmation

I feel good about myself because...

Today, I forgive myself for...

Reflection

Reminder

WEEKLY SELF LOVE JOURNAL

Mood: ☹ ☹ 😐 ☺ 😀   Date:

Monday

Three positive things about me...

Tuesday

I feel good about myself when...

Wednesday

Things I should do when I'm sad...

Thursday

Things I should do when I'm Bored...

WEEKLY SELF LOVE JOURNAL

Mood: ☹ ☹ 😐 🙂 😀　　　Date:

Friday

Things I should do when I feel tired...

Saturday

Things that made me happy today...

Sunday

I will challenge myself to...

Notes:

DAILY SELF LOVE JOURNAL

Mood: 😞 ☹️ 😐 🙂 😃   Date:

Empowering
affirmation

I feel good about
myself because...

Today, I forgive
myself for...

Reflection

Reminder

WEEKLY SELF LOVE JOURNAL

Mood: 😞 😟 😐 🙂 😃   Date:

Monday

Three positive things about me...

Tuesday

I feel good about myself when...

Wednesday

Things I should do when I'm sad...

Thursday

Things I should do when I'm Bored...

WEEKLY SELF LOVE JOURNAL

Mood: ☹ ☹ 😐 ☺ 😃   Date:

Friday

Things I should do when I feel tired...

Saturday

Things that made me happy today...

Sunday

I will challenge myself to...

Notes:

DAILY SELF LOVE JOURNAL

Mood: 😦 😟 😐 🙂 😃   Date:

Empowering affirmation

I feel good about myself because...

Today, I forgive myself for...

Reflection

Reminder

____

____

____

____

____

____

____

____

WEEKLY SELF LOVE JOURNAL

Mood: 🙁 ☹️ 😐 🙂 😃   Date:

Monday

Three positive things about me...

Tuesday

I feel good about myself when...

Wednesday

Things I should do when I'm sad...

Thursday

Things I should do when I'm Bored...

WEEKLY SELF LOVE JOURNAL

Mood: ☹ ☹ 😐 🙂 😀   Date:

Friday

Things I should do when I feel tired...

Saturday

Things that made me happy today...

Sunday

I will challenge myself to...

Notes:

DAILY SELF LOVE JOURNAL

Mood: Date:

Empowering
affirmation

I feel good about
myself because...

Today, I forgive
myself for...

Reflection

Reminder

WEEKLY SELF LOVE JOURNAL

Mood: ☹ ☹ 😐 🙂 😃   Date:

Monday

Three positive things about me...

Tuesday

I feel good about myself when...

Wednesday

Things I should do when I'm sad...

Thursday

Things I should do when I'm Bored...

WEEKLY SELF LOVE JOURNAL

Mood: 😩 😔 😐 🙂 😃   Date:

Friday

Things I should do when I feel tired...

Saturday

Things that made me happy today...

Sunday

I will challenge myself to...

Notes:

DAILY SELF LOVE JOURNAL

Mood: ☹ ☹ 😐 🙂 😃   Date:

Empowering affirmation

I feel good about myself because...

Today, I forgive myself for...

Reflection

____

____

____

____

Reminder

____

____

____

____

WEEKLY SELF LOVE JOURNAL

Mood: ☹ ☹ 😐 ☺ 😃   Date:

Monday

Three positive things about me...

Tuesday

I feel good about myself when...

Wednesday

Things I should do when I'm sad...

Thursday

Things I should do when I'm Bored...

WEEKLY SELF LOVE JOURNAL

Mood: ☹ ☹ 😐 ☺ 😃   Date:

Friday

Things I should do when I feel tired...

Saturday

Things that made me happy today...

Sunday

I will challenge myself to...

Notes:

DAILY SELF LOVE JOURNAL

Mood: 😞 ☹️ 😐 🙂 😃　　　　Date:

Empowering affirmation

I feel good about myself because...

Today, I forgive myself for...

Reflection

Reminder

WEEKLY SELF LOVE JOURNAL

Mood: ☹ ☹ 😐 ☺ 😃   Date:

Monday

Three positive things about me...

Tuesday

I feel good about myself when...

Wednesday

Things I should do when I'm sad...

Thursday

Things I should do when I'm Bored...

WEEKLY SELF LOVE JOURNAL

Mood: ☹ ☹ 😐 ☺ 😃   Date:

Friday

Things I should do when I feel tired...

Saturday

Things that made me happy today...

Sunday

I will challenge myself to...

Notes:

DAILY SELF LOVE JOURNAL

Mood: ☹ ☹ 😐 🙂 😃   Date:

Empowering
affirmation

I feel good about
myself because...

Today, I forgive
myself for...

Reflection

Reminder

WEEKLY SELF LOVE JOURNAL

Mood: ☹ ☹ 😐 ☺ 😊   Date:

Monday

Three positive things about me...

Tuesday

I feel good about myself when...

Wednesday

Things I should do when I'm sad...

Thursday

Things I should do when I'm Bored...

WEEKLY SELF LOVE JOURNAL

Mood: ☹ ☹ 😐 ☺ 😄   Date:

Friday

Things I should do when I feel tired...

Saturday

Things that made me happy today...

Sunday

I will challenge myself to...

Notes:

DAILY SELF LOVE JOURNAL

Mood: ☹ ☹ 😐 ☺ 😃   Date:

Empowering affirmation

I feel good about myself because...

Today, I forgive myself for...

Reflection

Reminder

_______________________   _______________________

_______________________   _______________________

_______________________   _______________________

_______________________   _______________________

WEEKLY SELF LOVE JOURNAL

Mood: 😞 😟 😐 🙂 😃   Date:

Monday

Three positive things about me...

Tuesday

I feel good about myself when...

Wednesday

Things I should do when I'm sad...

Thursday

Things I should do when I'm Bored...

WEEKLY SELF LOVE JOURNAL

Mood: ☹ ☹ 😐 ☺ 😄   Date:

Friday

Things I should do when I feel tired...

Saturday

Things that made me happy today...

Sunday

I will challenge myself to...

Notes:

DAILY SELF LOVE JOURNAL

Mood: ☹ ☹ 😐 🙂 😀   Date:

Empowering affirmation

I feel good about myself because...

Today, I forgive myself for...

Reflection

Reminder

_______________   _______________

_______________   _______________

_______________   _______________

_______________   _______________

WEEKLY SELF LOVE JOURNAL

Mood: ☹ ☹ 😐 ☺ 😃   Date:

Monday

Three positive things about me...

Tuesday

I feel good about myself when...

Wednesday

Things I should do when I'm sad...

Thursday

Things I should do when I'm Bored...

WEEKLY SELF LOVE JOURNAL

Mood: 😞 😟 😐 🙂 😃   Date:

Friday

Things I should do when I feel tired...

Saturday

Things that made me happy today...

Sunday

I will challenge myself to...

Notes:

DAILY SELF LOVE JOURNAL

Mood: ☹ ☹ 😐 ☺ 😃   Date:

Empowering
affirmation

I feel good about
myself because...

Today, I forgive
myself for...

Reflection

Reminder

WEEKLY SELF LOVE JOURNAL

Mood: ☹ ☹ 😐 ☺ 😃   Date:

Monday

Three positive things about me...

Tuesday

I feel good about myself when...

Wednesday

Things I should do when I'm sad...

Thursday

Things I should do when I'm Bored...

WEEKLY SELF LOVE JOURNAL

Mood: 😖 😞 😐 🙂 😃   Date:

Friday

Things I should do when I feel tired...

Saturday

Things that made me happy today...

Sunday

I will challenge myself to...

Notes:

DAILY SELF LOVE JOURNAL

Mood: 😠 😞 😐 🙂 😄   Date:

Empowering affirmation

I feel good about myself because...

Today, I forgive myself for...

Reflection

Reminder

WEEKLY SELF LOVE JOURNAL

Mood: 😞 😟 😐 🙂 😄   Date:

Monday

Three positive things about me...

Tuesday

I feel good about myself when...

Wednesday

Things I should do when I'm sad...

Thursday

Things I should do when I'm Bored...

WEEKLY SELF LOVE JOURNAL

Mood: ☹ ☹ 😐 🙂 😄   Date:

Friday

Things I should do when I feel tired...

Saturday

Things that made me happy today...

Sunday

I will challenge myself to...

Notes:

DAILY SELF LOVE JOURNAL

Mood: ☹ ☹ 😐 🙂 😀   Date:

Empowering affirmation

I feel good about myself because...

Today, I forgive myself for...

Reflection

Reminder

WEEKLY SELF LOVE JOURNAL

Mood: ☹ ☹ 😐 ☺ 😃   Date:

Monday

Three positive things about me...

Tuesday

I feel good about myself when...

Wednesday

Things I should do when I'm sad...

Thursday

Things I should do when I'm Bored...

WEEKLY SELF LOVE JOURNAL

Mood: ☹ ☹ 😐 ☺ 😃   Date:

Friday

Things I should do when I feel tired...

Saturday

Things that made me happy today...

Sunday

I will challenge myself to...

Notes:

DAILY SELF LOVE JOURNAL

Mood: ☹ ☹ 😐 🙂 😃   Date:

Empowering affirmation

I feel good about myself because...

Today, I forgive myself for...

Reflection

Reminder

WEEKLY SELF LOVE JOURNAL

Mood: ☹ ☹ 😐 ☺ 😃   Date:

Monday

Three positive things about me...

Tuesday

I feel good about myself when...

Wednesday

Things I should do when I'm sad...

Thursday

Things I should do when I'm Bored...

WEEKLY SELF LOVE JOURNAL

Mood: ☹ ☹ 😐 ☺ 😃   Date:

Friday

Things I should do when I feel tired...

Saturday

Things that made me happy today...

Sunday

I will challenge myself to...

Notes:

DAILY SELF LOVE JOURNAL

Mood: ☹ ☹ 😐 ☺ 😀   **Date:**

Empowering affirmation

I feel good about myself because...

Today, I forgive myself for...

Reflection

____

____

____

____

Reminder

____

____

____

____

WEEKLY SELF LOVE JOURNAL

Mood: ☹ ☹ 😐 ☺ 😃   Date:

Monday

Three positive things about me...

Tuesday

I feel good about myself when...

Wednesday

Things I should do when I'm sad...

Thursday

Things I should do when I'm Bored...

WEEKLY SELF LOVE JOURNAL

Mood: ☹ ☹ 😐 🙂 😃   Date:

Friday

Things I should do when I feel tired...

Saturday

Things that made me happy today...

Sunday

I will challenge myself to...

Notes:

DAILY SELF LOVE JOURNAL

Mood: 😠 😞 😐 🙂 😄   Date:

Empowering affirmation

I feel good about myself because...

Today, I forgive myself for...

Reflection

Reminder

_______________________   _______________________

_______________________   _______________________

_______________________   _______________________

_______________________   _______________________

WEEKLY SELF LOVE JOURNAL

Mood: 🙁 ☹️ 😐 🙂 😃   Date:

Monday

Three positive things about me...

Tuesday

I feel good about myself when...

Wednesday

Things I should do when I'm sad...

Thursday

Things I should do when I'm Bored...

WEEKLY SELF LOVE JOURNAL

Mood: ☹ ☹ 😐 ☺ 😃   Date:

Friday

Things I should do when I feel tired...

Saturday

Things that made me happy today...

Sunday

I will challenge myself to...

Notes:

DAILY SELF LOVE JOURNAL

Mood: ☹ ☹ 😐 ☺ 😃   Date:

Empowering
affirmation

I feel good about
myself because...

Today, I forgive
myself for...

Reflection

Reminder

WEEKLY SELF LOVE JOURNAL

Mood: ☹ ☹ 😐 ☺ 😄   Date:

Monday

Three positive things about me...

Tuesday

I feel good about myself when...

Wednesday

Things I should do when I'm sad...

Thursday

Things I should do when I'm Bored...

WEEKLY SELF LOVE JOURNAL

Mood: ☹ ☹ 😐 ☺ 😃   Date:

Friday

Things I should do when I feel tired...

Saturday

Things that made me happy today...

Sunday

I will challenge myself to...

Notes:

DAILY SELF LOVE JOURNAL

Mood: ☹ ☹ 😐 ☺ 😄   Date:

Empowering affirmation

I feel good about myself because...

Today, I forgive myself for...

Reflection

Reminder

WEEKLY SELF LOVE JOURNAL

Mood: ☹ ☹ 😐 ☺ 😄   Date:

Monday

Three positive things about me...

Tuesday

I feel good about myself when...

Wednesday

Things I should do when I'm sad...

Thursday

Things I should do when I'm Bored...

WEEKLY SELF LOVE JOURNAL

Mood: 🙁 🙁 😐 🙂 😄   Date:

Friday

Things I should do when I feel tired...

Saturday

Things that made me happy today...

Sunday

I will challenge myself to...

Notes:

DAILY SELF LOVE JOURNAL

Mood: ☹ ☹ 😐 ☺ 😃   Date:

Empowering affirmation

I feel good about myself because...

Today, I forgive myself for...

Reflection

Reminder

WEEKLY SELF LOVE JOURNAL

Mood: 😦 😦 😐 🙂 😃   Date:

Monday

Three positive things about me...

Tuesday

I feel good about myself when...

Wednesday

Things I should do when I'm sad...

Thursday

Things I should do when I'm Bored...

WEEKLY SELF LOVE JOURNAL

Mood: ☹ ☹ 😐 ☺ 😃   Date:

Friday

Things I should do when I feel tired...

Saturday

Things that made me happy today...

Sunday

I will challenge myself to...

Notes:

DAILY SELF LOVE JOURNAL

Mood: ☹ ☹ 😐 ☺ 😃   Date:

Empowering affirmation

I feel good about myself because...

Today, I forgive myself for...

Reflection

Reminder

WEEKLY SELF LOVE JOURNAL

Mood: 😞 😟 😐 ☺ 😃   Date:

Monday

Three positive things about me...

Tuesday

I feel good about myself when...

Wednesday

Things I should do when I'm sad...

Thursday

Things I should do when I'm Bored...

WEEKLY SELF LOVE JOURNAL

| Mood: ☹ ☹ ☺ ☺ ☺ | Date: |

Friday

Things I should do when I feel tired...

Saturday

Things that made me happy today...

Sunday

I will challenge myself to...

Notes:

DAILY SELF LOVE JOURNAL

Mood: ☹ ☹ 😐 ☺ 😃   Date:

Empowering affirmation

I feel good about myself because...

Today, I forgive myself for...

Reflection

Reminder

WEEKLY SELF LOVE JOURNAL

Mood: 🙁 ☹️ 😐 🙂 😃   Date:

Monday

Three positive things about me...

Tuesday

I feel good about myself when...

Wednesday

Things I should do when I'm sad...

Thursday

Things I should do when I'm Bored...

WEEKLY SELF LOVE JOURNAL

Mood: ☹ ☹ 😐 ☺ 😄   Date:

Friday

Things I should do when I feel tired...

Saturday

Things that made me happy today...

Sunday

I will challenge myself to...

Notes:

DAILY SELF LOVE JOURNAL

Mood: ☹ ☹ 😐 ☺ 😃   Date:

Empowering
affirmation

I feel good about
myself because...

Today, I forgive
myself for...

Reflection

Reminder

WEEKLY SELF LOVE JOURNAL

Mood: ☹ ☹ 😐 ☺ 😃   Date:

Monday

Three positive things about me...

Tuesday

I feel good about myself when...

Wednesday

Things I should do when I'm sad...

Thursday

Things I should do when I'm Bored...

WEEKLY SELF LOVE JOURNAL

Mood: ☹ ☹ 😐 ☺ 😃　　　　Date:

Friday

Things I should do when I feel tired...

Saturday

Things that made me happy today...

Sunday

I will challenge myself to...

Notes:

DAILY SELF LOVE JOURNAL

Mood: 😟 😦 😐 🙂 😃   Date:

Empowering affirmation

I feel good about myself because...

Today, I forgive myself for...

Reflection

Reminder

WEEKLY SELF LOVE JOURNAL

Mood: ☹ ☹ 😐 🙂 😃   Date:

Monday

Three positive things about me...

Tuesday

I feel good about myself when...

Wednesday

Things I should do when I'm sad...

Thursday

Things I should do when I'm Bored...

WEEKLY SELF LOVE JOURNAL

Mood: ☹ ☹ 😐 ☺ 😄   Date:

Friday

Things I should do when I feel tired...

Saturday

Things that made me happy today...

Sunday

I will challenge myself to...

Notes:

DAILY SELF LOVE JOURNAL

Mood: ☹ ☹ 😐 🙂 😀   Date:

Empowering affirmation

I feel good about myself because...

Today, I forgive myself for...

Reflection

Reminder

WEEKLY SELF LOVE JOURNAL

Mood: ☹ ☹ 😐 ☺ 😃   Date:

Monday

Three positive things about me...

Tuesday

I feel good about myself when...

Wednesday

Things I should do when I'm sad...

Thursday

Things I should do when I'm Bored...

WEEKLY SELF LOVE JOURNAL

Mood: 🙁 ☹️ 😐 🙂 😃   Date:

Friday

Things I should do when I feel tired...

Saturday

Things that made me happy today...

Sunday

I will challenge myself to...

Notes:

DAILY SELF LOVE JOURNAL

Mood: 😟 😦 😐 🙂 😀   Date:

Empowering affirmation

I feel good about myself because...

Today, I forgive myself for...

Reflection

Reminder

WEEKLY SELF LOVE JOURNAL

Mood: 😟 😦 😐 🙂 😃　　　Date:

Monday

Three positive things about me...

Tuesday

I feel good about myself when...

Wednesday

Things I should do when I'm sad...

Thursday

Things I should do when I'm Bored...

WEEKLY SELF LOVE JOURNAL

Mood: ☹ ☹ 😐 ☺ 😃   Date:

Friday

Things I should do when I feel tired...

Saturday

Things that made me happy today...

Sunday

I will challenge myself to...

Notes:

DAILY SELF LOVE JOURNAL

Mood: ☹ ☹ 😐 ☺ 😄   Date:

Empowering affirmation

I feel good about myself because...

Today, I forgive myself for...

Reflection

Reminder

WEEKLY SELF LOVE JOURNAL

Mood: ☹ ☹ 😐 ☺ 😃   Date:

Monday

Three positive things about me...

Tuesday

I feel good about myself when...

Wednesday

Things I should do when I'm sad...

Thursday

Things I should do when I'm Bored...

WEEKLY SELF LOVE JOURNAL

Mood: ☹ ☹ 😐 ☺ 😃   Date:

Friday

Things I should do when I feel tired...

Saturday

Things that made me happy today...

Sunday

I will challenge myself to...

Notes:

DAILY SELF LOVE JOURNAL

Mood: Date:

Empowering
affirmation

I feel good about
myself because...

Today, I forgive
myself for...

Reflection

Reminder

WEEKLY SELF LOVE JOURNAL

Mood: ☹ ☹ 😐 ☺ 😃   Date:

Monday

Three positive things about me...

Tuesday

I feel good about myself when...

Wednesday

Things I should do when I'm sad...

Thursday

Things I should do when I'm Bored...

WEEKLY SELF LOVE JOURNAL

Mood: ☹ ☹ 😐 ☺ 😃   Date:

Friday

Things I should do when I feel tired...

Saturday

Things that made me happy today...

Sunday

I will challenge myself to...

Notes:

SELF LOVE
JOURNAL
Book Club